THE ELTON JOHN COLLECTION

ISBN 0-7935-4719-9

HAL•LEONARD® CORPORATION
7777 W. BLUEMOUND RD. P.O. BOX 13819 MILWAUKEE, WI 53213

BELIEVE

Words and Music by ELTON JOHN
and BERNIE TAUPIN

Slow Rock ballad

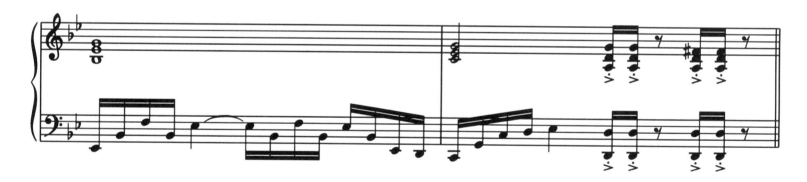

6

BENNIE AND THE JETS

Words and Music by ELTON JOHN
and BERNIE TAUPIN

Moderately, in 2

To Coda ⊕

BLUE EYES

Words and Music by ELTON JOHN
and GARY OSBORNE

BORDER SONG

Words and Music by ELTON JOHN
and BERNIE TAUPIN

Slowly, with a beat

D.S. al Coda

CODA

CANDLE IN THE WIND

Words and Music by ELTON JOHN
and BERNIE TAUPIN

CIRCLE OF LIFE

Music by ELTON JOHN
Lyrics by TIM RICE

Relaxed pop beat

CROCODILE ROCK

Words and Music by ELTON JOHN
and BERNIE TAUPIN

Light-hearted Rock

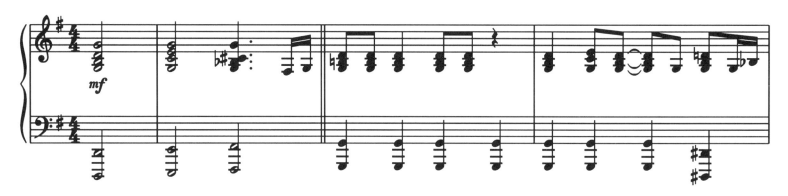

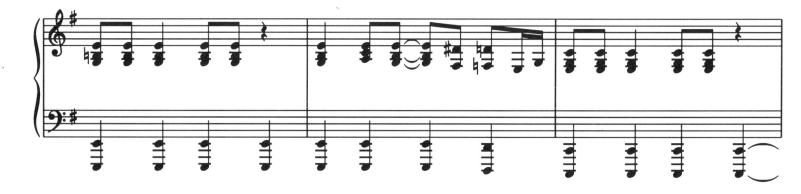

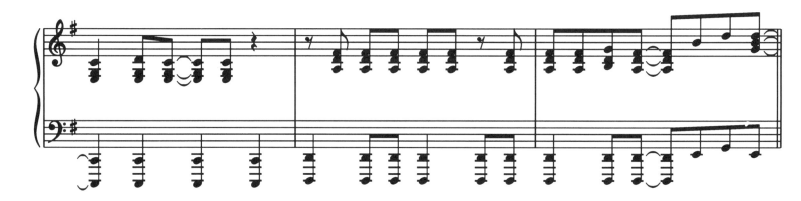

To Coda

CAN YOU FEEL THE LOVE TONIGHT
from Walt Disney Pictures' THE LION KING

Music by ELTON JOHN
Lyrics by TIM RICE

DANIEL

Words and Music by ELTON JOHN
and BERNIE TAUPIN

Moderately bright

To Coda

DON'T LET THE SUN GO DOWN ON ME

Words and Music by ELTON JOHN
and BERNIE TAUPIN

EMPTY GARDEN
(HEY HEY JOHNNY)

Words and Music by ELTON JOHN
and BERNIE TAUPIN

Gentle Rock

HONKY CAT

Words and Music by ELTON JOHN
and BERNIE TAUPIN

Brightly, with spirit

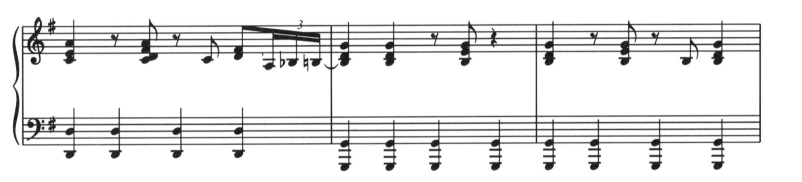

GOODBYE YELLOW BRICK ROAD

Words and Music by ELTON JOHN
and BERNIE TAUPIN

Moderately slow, in 2

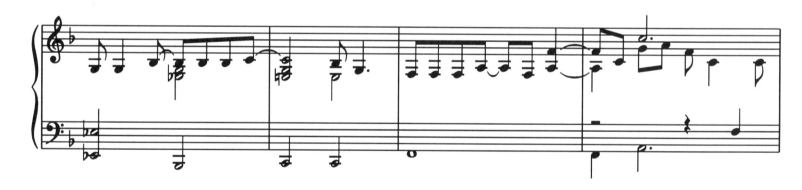

D.S. al Coda

CODA

rit.

I GUESS THAT'S WHY THEY CALL IT THE BLUES

Words and Music by ELTON JOHN,
BERNIE TAUPIN and DAVEY JOHNSTONE

LEVON

Moderately slow, with a beat

Words and Music by ELTON JOHN
and BERNIE TAUPIN

With pedal

THE LAST SONG

Words and Music by ELTON JOHN
and BERNIE TAUPIN

ROCKET MAN
(I Think It's Gonna Be A Long Long Time)

Words and Music by ELTON JOHN
and BERNIE TAUPIN

Moderately slow, with a beat

THE ONE

Words and Music by ELTON JOHN
and BERNIE TAUPIN

SAD SONGS
(Say So Much)

Words and Music by ELTON JOHN
and BERNIE TAUPIN

Moderately, with a blues feel

SOMEONE SAVED MY LIFE TONIGHT

Words and Music by ELTON JOHN
and BERNIE TAUPIN

Slowly

YOUR SONG

Words and Music by ELTON JOHN
and BERNIE TAUPIN

Moderately slow, in 2

SACRIFICE

Words and Music by ELTON JOHN
and BERNIE TAUPIN

Slowly

With pedal

D.S. al Coda

CODA

rit.

Contemporary Classics
Your favorite songs for piano, voice and guitar.

The Definitive Rock 'n' Roll Collection
A classic collection of the best songs from the early rock 'n' roll years – 1955-1966. 97 songs, including: Barbara Ann • Chantilly Lace • Dream Lover • Duke Of Earl • Earth Angel • Great Balls Of Fire • Louie, Louie • Rock Around The Clock • Ruby Baby • Runaway • (Seven Little Girls) Sitting In The Back Seat • Stay • Surfin' U.S.A. • Wild Thing • Woolly Bully • and more.
00490195 ....$27.95

The Big Book Of Rock
78 of rock's biggest hits, including: Addicted To Love • American Pie • Born To Be Wild • Cold As Ice • Dust In The Wind • Free Bird • Goodbye Yellow Brick Road • Groovin' • Hey Jude • I Love Rock N Roll • Lay Down Sally • Layla • Livin' On A Prayer • Louie Louie • Maggie May • Me And Bobby McGee • Monday, Monday • Owner Of A Lonely Heart • Shout • Walk This Way • We Didn't Start The Fire • You Really Got Me • and more.
00311566..$19.95

Big Book Of Movie And TV Themes
Over 90 familiar themes, including: Alfred Hitchcock Theme • Beauty And The Beast • Candle On The Water • Theme From *E.T.* • Endless Love • Hawaii Five-O • I Love Lucy • Theme From *Jaws* • Jetsons • Major Dad Theme • The Masterpiece • Mickey Mouse March • The Munsters Theme • Theme From *Murder, She Wrote* • Mystery • Somewhere Out There • Unchained Melody • Won't You Be My Neighbor • and more!
00311582 ....$19.95

The Best Rock Songs Ever
70 of the best rock songs from yesterday and today, including: All Day And All Of The Night • All Shook Up • Ballroom Blitz • Bennie And The Jets • Blue Suede Shoes • Born To Be Wild • Boys Are Back In Town • Every Breath You Take • Faith • Free Bird • Hey Jude • I Still Haven't Found What I'm Looking For • Livin' On A Prayer • Lola • Louie Louie • Maggie May • Money • (She's) Some Kind Of Wonderful • Takin' Care Of Business • Walk This Way • We Didn't Start The Fire • We Got The Beat • Wild Thing • more!
00490424 ....$16.95

The Best Of 90s Rock
30 songs, including: Alive • I'd Do Anything For Love (But I Won't Do That) • Livin' On The Edge • Losing My Religion • Two Princes • Walking On Broken Glass • Wind Of Change • and more.
00311668 ....$14.95

35 Classic Hits
35 contemporary favorites, including: Beauty And The Beast • Dust In The Wind • Just The Way You Are • Moon River • The River Of Dreams • Somewhere Out There • Tears In Heaven • When I Fall In Love • A Whole New World (Aladdin's Theme) • and more.
00311654 ....$12.95

55 Contemporary Standards
55 favorites, including: Alfie • Beauty And The Beast • Can't Help Falling In Love • Candle In The Wind • Have I Told You Lately • How Am I Supposed To Live Without You • Memory • The River Of Dreams • Sea Of Love • Tears In Heaven • Up Where We Belong • When I Fall In Love • and more.
00311670 ....$15.95

Women of Modern Rock
25 songs from contemporary chanteuses, including: As I Lay Me Down • Connection • Feed The Tree • Galileo • Here And Now • Look What Love Has Done • Love Sneakin' Up On You • Walking On Broken Glass • You Oughta Know • Zombie • and more.
00310093 ....$14.95

Jock Rock Hits
32 stadium-shaking favorites, including: Another One Bites The Dust • The Boys Are Back In Town • Freeze-Frame • Gonna Make You Sweat (Everybody Dance Now) • I Got You (I Feel Good) • Na Na Hey Hey Kiss Him Goodbye • Rock & Roll – Part II (The Hey Song) • Shout • Tequila • We Are The Champions • We Will Rock You • Whoomp! (There It Is) • Wild Thing • and more.
00310105 ....$14.95

Rock Ballads
31 sentimental favorites, including: All For Love • Bed Of Roses • Dust In The Wind • Everybody Hurts • Right Here Waiting • Tears In Heaven • and more.
00311673 ....$14.95

0997

Your Favorite Music Arranged For Piano Solo

Classic Broadway Solos
16 beautifully arranged Broadway standards including: I Could Have Danced All Night • If Ever I Would Leave You • The Impossible Dream • Memory • Smoke Gets In Your Eyes • You'll Never Walk Alone • and more.
00294002........$10.95

Opera At The Movies
22 operatic favorites from *Amadeus, Apocalypse Now, Breaking Away, Chariots Of Fire, Fatal Attraction, Godfather III, Moonstruck, Pretty Woman*, and more.
00292028.........$8.95

Classical Themes from The Movies
Over 30 familiar and favorite themes, including: Also Sprach Zarathustra • Ave Maria • Canon In D • Love Duet (from *La Bohème*) • Overture To The Marriage Of Figaro • and more.
00221010............................$9.95

Andrew Lloyd Webber For Piano
14 pieces, including: All I Ask Of You • Don't Cry For Me Argentina • Memory • and more.
00292001........$10.95

Jazz Favorites
15 songs, including: April In Paris • Body And Soul • Have You Met Miss Jones? • My Favorite Things • A Night In Tunisia • Sophisticated Lady • and more.
00292054........$12.95

Jazz Standards
15 all-time favorite songs, including: All The Things You Are • Bluesette • I'll Remember April • Mood Indigo • Satin Doll • and more.
00292055.........$12.95

Love & Wedding Piano Solos
26 contemporary and classic wedding favorites, including: All I Ask Of You • Ave Maria • Endless Love • Through The Years • Vision Of Love • Sunrise, Sunset • Don't Know Much • Unchained Melody • and more.
00311507............................$12.95

The Lion King
7 piano solos featuring: Circle Of Life • I Just Can't Wait To Be King • Be Prepared • Can You Feel The Love Tonight • and more.
00292060........$10.95

Movie Piano Solos
20 rich arrangements, including: The Exodus Song • The Firm Main Title • The Godfather (Love Theme) • Moon River • Raider's March • Theme From Schindler's List • When I Fall In Love • A Whole New World • and more.
00311675............................$9.95

TV Themes
33 classic themes, including: Addams Family • Alfred Hitchcock Presents • Dinosaurs • (Meet) The Flintstones • Home Improvement • Northern Exposure • Mystery • This Is It (Bugs Bunny Theme) • Twin Peaks • and more!
00292030............................$9.95

Narada New Age Piano Sampler
A unique collection of 17 pieces by five different artists as represented by Narada Records, one of the premier new age record labels. Artists include: David Lanz, Michael Jones, Spencer Brewer, Richard Souther, Wayne Gratz.
00490211............................$10.95

Windham Hill Piano Sampler
This book features a sampling of ten popular Windham Hill recording artists, including: Philip Aaberg, Scott Cossu, Malcolm Dalglish, Barbara Higbie, Triona Ni Dhomhnaill, Bill Quist, Fred Simon, Ira Stein, Liz Story, and Tim Story. It is complete with biographies and discographies for each artist as well as an introduction about the Windham Hill record labels. 18 pieces in all.
00312484............................$14.95

Sacred Inspirations
arr. *Phillip Keveren*
11 songs, featuring: El Shaddai • Great Is The Lord • Amazing Grace • Friends • Place In This World • and more.
00292057............................$9.95

Piano Solo Favorites
20 arrangements, including: Born Free • Chariots Of Fire • Just The Way You Are • Unexpected Song • The Way We Were • and more.
00292068........$12.95

Elvis Presley Piano Solos
A great collection of over 15 of The King's best, including: Are You Lonesome Tonight? • Don't Be Cruel • It's Now Or Never • Love Me Tender • All Shook Up • and more!
00292002............................$8.95

Prices, contents, and availability subject to change without notice. Some products may not be available outside the U.S.A.